THE CHANGING FACE OF THE
NETHERLANDS

Text and Photographs
by DAVID SIMSON

Chicago, Illinois

© 2005 Raintree

Published by Raintree, a division of Reed Elsevier, Inc.
Chicago, Illinois
Customer Service 888-363-4266
Visit our website at www.raintreelibrary.com

For information address the publisher:
Raintree
100 N. LaSalle
Suite 1200
Chicago, IL 60602

Library of Congress Cataloging-in-Publication Data:

Simson, David.
  The Netherlands / David Simson.
      p. cm. -- (Changing face of--)
Summary: Presents the natural environment and resources, people and
culture, and business and economy of The Netherlands, focusing on
development and change in recent years.
Includes bibliographical references and index.
  ISBN 0-7398-6833-0
  1. Netherlands--Juvenile literature. [1. Netherlands.] I. Title. II.
Series.
  DJ18.S55 2004
  949.2--dc21

                            2003009746

Printed in China, bound in the United States.

08 07 06 05 04
10 9 8 7 6 5 4 3 2 1

Acknowledgments
The publishers would like to thank
the following for their contributions
to this book: Rob Bowden—statistics
research; Peter Bull—map illustration;
and Nick Hawken—statistics panel
illustrations. All photographs are by
David Simson.

Contents

Rotterdam: The Reborn City

Rotterdam, now a bustling city of 600,000 people, was once a small settlement built on the Rotte River in about 1270 C.E. It grew slowly over the centuries—in the 1400s, for instance, when neighboring Delft was an important city, Rotterdam was still a very small town. In 1872 a new canal was built that linked two of the great rivers of Europe and flowed into the sea at Rotterdam. This canal made Rotterdam an important center for trade and industry, and the city became very wealthy.

In 1940 Hitler invaded the Netherlands. Most of the buildings in Rotterdam were completely demolished. At the end of World War II, in 1945, Het Schielandshuis was one of the only historic buildings left standing. Originally a government office, it is now Rotterdam's Historic Museum.

Rotterdam was entirely rebuilt after the war. Its modern architecture, such as the Erasmus Bridge and the Cubehouses, has become world renowned. Modern shopping malls have replaced more traditional shopping areas, and the world's largest port, the Europoort, has been built at Rotterdam.

Due to its central position in Europe and excellent transportation links, Rotterdam has become a center for Internet companies and other businesses. The Dutch-owned multinational company Unilever has its headquarters in the city. Several Shell oil refineries and well-known companies such as IBM, Toshiba, and Microsoft all do business there. As the European Union expands, Rotterdam—like the Netherlands itself—should enjoy continued prosperity.

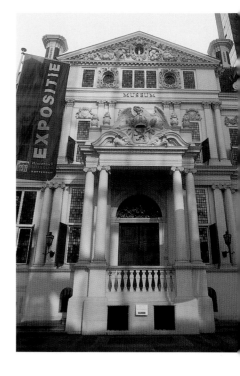

▲ *The Rotterdam Historic Museum, Het Schielandshuis, is a reminder of the people of Rotterdam's resilience in times of adversity.*

◄ *The Erasmus Bridge is an example of the stunning modern architecture in the city of Rotterdam. Barges and ships travel nonstop between the Europoort on the coast through the city of Rotterdam into the heartland of Europe.*

▲ *This map shows the main geographical features of the Netherlands as well as most of the places mentioned in this book.*

THE NETHERLANDS: KEY FACTS

Area: 16,033 sq mi (41,526 sq km); 13,107 sq mi (33,948 sq km) excluding water

Population: 16.07 million

Population density: 183 people per sq mi (473 people per sq km)

Capital city: Amsterdam

Other main cities: The Hague, Utrecht, Eindhoven, Tilburg

Lowest point: Zuidplaspolder 23 ft (7 m)

Highest point: Vaalserberg 1,053 ft (321 m)

Longest river: Meuse 343 yd (314 km)

Main language: Dutch

Major religions: Roman Catholic 31 percent, Protestant 21 percent, Muslim 4.4 percent, other 3.6 percent, unaffiliated 40 percent

Currency: Euro

2 Past Times

The people and language of the Netherlands are known in English as "Dutch." Dutch comes from the German word for German, *Deutsch*. The majority of the Dutch population is of Germanic heritage. In the Netherlands they call themselves *Nederlanders* and their language *Nederlands*.

The area was first inhabited by Celtic and Germanic tribes. In the 1400s the area came under the control of the Austro-Hungarian Empire, and in the 1500s it was taken over by Spain. A war of independence from Spain was waged for 80 years, and independence was finally won in 1648. The years 1600–1700 are known as the "Golden Age" of Dutch history. This was a period of unusual wealth and freedom for the country. Belgium and Luxembourg were part of the Netherlands at that time, and the country became a "colonial power," meaning that it controlled other less-powerful areas in the world, where it had trade interests.

▲ *The Royal Palace in Amsterdam was first used as the City Hall in 1655. It reflected the wealth of the city.*

▼ *Even though the capital of the Netherlands is Amsterdam, the Binnenhof, the historic Dutch Parliament buildings, have been in The Hague since the 1500s.*

In 1795 the Netherlands came under the control of France, and in 1815 independence was restored. The Netherlands stayed neutral during World War I (1914–1918), but it was invaded by Nazi Germany during World War II (1939–1945). Although the Netherlands had a tradition of neutrality, in 1949 it joined NATO, and in 1957 it became one of the founding members of the European Economic Community.

Today, the Netherlands's government is a constitutional monarchy. This means that, although there is a monarch (Queen Beatrix since 1980), the country is a democracy.

▶ *Queen Beatrix attending the signing of the Treaty of Maastricht in 1991.*

IN THEIR OWN WORDS

My name is Jelle van der Beek. I am 16 and go to school in Tilburg. Sometimes I work in a trendy clothes boutique in the city to make pocket money. My favorite subject is history. In Dutch schools, European history and international history are taught alongside Dutch history. It gives us a wider view of the world. Many people do not know, for instance, that New York's original name was New Amsterdam because the Dutch were the first people to settle there. And Harlem was named after Haarlem in Holland. The first European navigator to discover New Zealand was a Dutchmen named Abel Tasman, not Captain Cook. Tasmania and the Tasman sea were named after him. New Zealand was named after the Dutch province of Zeeland.

Landscape and Climate

The Netherlands is bordered by Belgium, Germany, and the North Sea, and it has a total land area of 13,107 sq mi (33,948 sq km). It is a very flat, low-lying country. The estuaries of two major rivers, the Meuse and the Schelde, are in the Netherlands, and the land is crisscrossed by rivers, canals, and drainage ditches. Thirty percent of the land is below sea level, so floods are a great danger. Huge sand dunes help to protect the land. Where there are no dunes, artificial sea defenses, called dikes, have been built, such as the 19-mi (30-km) *Afsluitdijk* (shut-off dike), the North Holland Seawall (running south of Den Helder), and sea locks such as the Zeeland Delta Project. A complicated drainage system helps to prevent flooding inland on the polders.

▼ *Coarse grasses are grown on the natural sand dunes at Brouwersdam in the Zeeland Delta region to hold the sand in place.*

Polders

Polders make up large areas of the Netherlands. A polder is an area of land that has been reclaimed from the sea. The process of making a polder is very involved. First, a dike is built that encloses a large area of the sea, and water is pumped out of this area until it is completely dry. In the past windmills were used for this task. Coarse grasses are then planted, which help to hold the soil and reduce the salt content. This whole

IN THEIR OWN WORDS

My name is Binne Kunnen and I'm 61 years old. I am originally a farmer's son from Friesland. I am a farmer now, but I live in another province called Flevoland. Forty years ago Flevoland did not exist because it was underwater. This area used to be a large bay in the North Sea called the Zuiderzee. After the building of the *Afsluitdijk* it became a large lake called the IJsselmeer. It has been gradually dried out to become the largest polder in the Netherlands, large enough to become a new province. If we had been standing here 40 years ago, we would have been on the ocean floor under more than 15 feet of water! Today we grow wheat, onions, potatoes, carrots, and, of course, tulips on this land.

process takes several years, and fertilizers must be used before the land can be used as productive farmland. Sections of the IJsselmeer have been dried out to create a new province of the Netherlands, known as Flevoland.

▼ *New housing estates, some with their own boat jetties, have been built in the new city of Lelystad, on the large Flevoland polder.*

Islands and heathlands

Along the full length of the North Sea coast, which is 400 mi (643 km), there are beautiful sandy beaches backed by high dunes and artificial sea defenses. Just off the north coast there is a line of low sandy islands called the Wadden Islands. These are important breeding sites for birds, and they are also popular with tourists.

The Hoge Veluwe, near the eastern border with Germany, is the Netherlands' largest national park. It is an area of forest, sand, and heathland where red deer and wild boar can sometimes be spotted.

The hilly south

Limburg, in the southeast of the country, is different from the rest of the Netherlands because it is hilly. The two countries that border the Netherlands, Germany and Belgium, meet here at a point called the *Drielandenpunt* ("Point of Three Countries"). The Vaalserberg, located here, is the highest point in the Netherlands.

▲ *An avenue of large oak trees in the Hoge Veluwe National Park, in the eastern Netherlands.*

▼ *The hilly orchard and meadow land of South Limburg.*

IN THEIR OWN WORDS

I'm Sander Kroonen and I am 14. I live at Vaals on the border of both Germany and Belgium. The borders of these two countries and Belgium meet here at the *Drielandenpunt*, the highest point in the Netherlands. My mom comes from here. My father is actually Belgian. He now works in Aachen, a city in neighboring Germany, only fifteen minutes away. The *Drielandenpunt* is a great place to go exploring. Only a few years ago you couldn't go there without a passport or identity papers. There used to be a staffed border control, but now there isn't even a border post. Everyone used to have to change money. Now we all use the euro.

The Netherlands Antilles

The Netherlands Antilles is a group of tropical islands in the Caribbean. Aruba, Bonaire, and Curaçao are flat, dry islands off the Venezuelan coast. Saint Eustatius, Saba, and part of Saint Martin in the Leeward Islands are volcanic and mountainous. The Antilles were once colonies of the Netherlands. Today they have complete control of their internal affairs. The Netherlands is responsible for their foreign affairs.

▶ *The main beach at Philipsburg on Saint Martin in the Netherlands Antilles. This island is controlled by both the French and the Dutch.*

Mild, wet, and windy

The climate of the Netherlands is typical of the northern European North Sea coast. It is mild and very wet, with a yearly average rainfall of 3 in. (76 mm). In the summer the temperatures rarely rise very high, and mid-winter temperatures usually remain above zero. In northern Holland the average January temperature is 41 °F (5 °C), and in July the average is 70 °F (21 °C). Further inland the weather tends to be drier, with some snow in the winter and higher temperatures in the summer.

▲ *The view of windmills and canals has become the accepted typical Dutch landscape, although modern postcards often have wind turbines on them.*

Wind blows in from the ocean and sweeps across the flat countryside. When there is no wind, a thick fog often covers the entire country. In summer it usually clears by late morning, and the rest of the day is beautifully sunny. In winter, a misty morning usually turns into a gray, dull day.

◀ *The Kite Festival on Scheveningen Beach near The Hague takes advantage of the sandy beaches and the almost constant windy conditions.*

Changing climate

The climate of the Netherlands has changed over the years—it has been getting much warmer. There is a famous 124-mi (200-km) ice-skating race, called the Elfstedentocht, that takes place on the canals through eleven towns in Friesland and attracts up to 18,000 people from all over the country. At the end of the 19th century this race took place almost every year, once the canals had frozen solid. These days the canals do not freeze up like they used to, and now the race only takes place about once every five years.

▶ *The Sint (saint) Servaas Bridge over the Meuse River at Maastricht. In the south, the weather tends to have colder winters and hotter summers.*

IN THEIR OWN WORDS

My name is René Waleson. I am 40 and am a technician at one of the Rotterdam Water Board's plants. This plant cleans all the household and factory wastewater from a large area of Rotterdam. After cleaning, this water is put back in the river. We actually clean 26 million gallons (100 million liters) of wastewater every day. That is the same as 35 Olympic swimming pools. The Water Boards do a very important job. They control water pollution, the construction and maintenance of dikes, and general water levels to prevent flooding. In the floods of January 1953, thousands of people died when water rose too high and flooded large areas of the country. It is the Water Board's job to prevent this from ever happening again.

4

Natural Resources

Gas and oil

Gas and oil were discovered offshore in the late 1960s. Many industries have developed to process the fuel or make oil-based products such as plastics and textiles. Ninety-five percent of all household energy requirements in the Netherlands are provided by natural gas. The country also makes more money from exporting gas than from any other product. Fifty percent of all Dutch gas is exported.

◀ *A North Sea oil rig is repaired in Rotterdam's Europoort. Once repaired, the rig will then be towed out to sea again to extract oil and gas from the seabed of the North Sea.*

▼ *A large wind farm near Zurich in Friesland. Wind power is considered very important in this windy country, even though it only produces a very small part of the nation's energy.*

Wind power

Wind power has been an important energy source in the Netherlands for centuries. Windmills were used in the past for pumping out water from the polders, grinding wheat, pulping paper, and making linseed oil. Now wind turbines are used to produce electricity for the nation, and there are many wind farms.

IN THEIR OWN WORDS

I'm Femke Klapwijk. I am 14 and I go to the Goes Lyceum school. But I live here in Colijnsplaat, a beautiful little Zeeland fishing village with fishing boats and windmills. It used to be on the sea, but then the Delta Project Sea Locks were built, and now the trawlers have to go through a lock to get to the sea. My father is a trawlerman and works out in the North Sea every day. He mainly fishes for sole, plaice, dab, cod, and eels. On the weekends I work at a wharfside fish store. Many people from as far away as Rotterdam come and buy fish here. We sell a lot of mussels, too, mainly to Belgians who come across the ferry at Breskens.

Fishing

The fishing industry has had difficulties in recent years. The European Union restricts the quota (amount) of fish that each country can catch. The quotas are being reduced because of concerns that the numbers of fish in the North Sea are falling. Pollution is one of the causes of this. However, the Zeeland mussel industry is thriving. This is mainly due to a healthy demand in northern Europe, particularly in Belgium, where a plate of mussels is a favorite national dish.

▼ *Urk was a famous seaport for over 700 years. Now the port is more than 31 mi (50 km) inland, on the IJsselmeer, a long way from open sea.*

Dairy and livestock

Almost half the land area of the
Netherlands is used for farming, with
most of this used for raising livestock.
The Dutch dairy industry is one of the
most efficient in the world, producing
large quantities of milk, butter, and
cheese, as well as many by-products,
such as yogurt, powdered milk, and
ingredients for factory-produced, ready-
made meals. Beef, pork, and chicken are
also important farm products in the
Netherlands.

▲ *Cheeses being sold at Alkmaar.
In the Netherlands, there is plenty
of fresh milk, butter, and cheese.*

◄ *There are many new farming
practices, from the use of
computer-run greenhouses and
eco-farming to the rearing of
bison, as on this farm in the
southern part of the country.*

Crops and horticulture

The Netherlands is famous for its tulips, and the flower
industry is one of the most advanced and profitable in
the world. Flowers from the Netherlands are flown daily
to flower markets worldwide. The industry's success is based
on the use of the latest scientific techniques and automated
production, which ensures that the plants get exactly the
growing conditions they need. This is also the case with
market gardening. Millions of computer-controlled

greenhouses in the Westland produce high-quality vegetables all year round, even outside their normal growing seasons. The Netherlands achieves some of the highest yields in fruit, flowers, and vegetables of any country in the world.

New crops such as rapeseed, which is used to produce vegetable oil, have been introduced. There is a move toward more organic farming, and the use of genetically engineered crops is an important new development.

▲ *The Netherlands has a great horticultural industry. These flowers will be sold at a flower auction in Aalsmeer, where the largest and most successful flower auctions in the world are held.*

IN THEIR OWN WORDS

I'm Albert Buining. I'm 35 and I work as a security man at the famous Aalsmeer Flower Auction, the largest in the world. It is a strange auction. Instead of the price going up, it starts high and goes down. Then, the buyer presses his bell when he wants to purchase that batch of flowers. It is very exciting. If you press your bell too late you lose the flowers to another buyer. If you press it too early, you pay too much. Then the flowers are delivered all over the world, many by air. Apart from general security, we also look after the many tourists that visit us to see the auction for themselves.

5

The Changing Environment

Recycling in industry

The need to recycle, reprocess, and reuse materials is being taken very seriously. It is changing the lifestyle of the Dutch as they enter the 21st century. The Dutch government has passed many laws to try to stop industries from dumping toxic and non-toxic waste. There is a determined effort to get industry to use reprocessed materials—for example, recycled materials are used for road surfacing. In every town there is a center where reclaimed building materials are sold to the building trade.

▲ *Fast-food restaurants take cleaning both in and around their establishments very seriously. Here, in Flevoland, an employee even clears a nearby forest of garbage.*

Recycling at home

There are "eco-taxes" on any product that is considered to be bad for the environment. People have to pay a deposit on bottles, even plastic ones, which they get back if they return the empty bottles to the store. On many household machines such as vacuum cleaners there is now a "reprocessing deposit," which is returned if people bring it back to the store when the machine no longer works or is out of date. Many stores have collection boxes for old batteries, while other stores no longer give out free plastic bags. People are obliged to sort and separate their garbage at home so that the different materials can be recycled.

▶ *Home garbage is sorted into recyclable material, biodegradable items, and general waste.*

Reuse

Secondhand stores recycle anything from clothes to furniture. *Snuffelmarkt* (flea markets) and street markets are good places to find secondhand goods, and many town councils have stores in which they resell items that were thrown out in the garbage. On Koninginnedag (Queen's Day), which is April 30, everyone in the country is invited to sell things they do not need in front of their house, turning the whole country into a massive flea market.

▶ *A secondhand street market near Callantsoog in North Holland.*

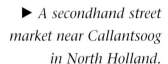

IN THEIR OWN WORDS

My name is Marloes Wolter, I am a 25-year-old teacher. In the Netherlands ecology is taken very seriously. There are all types of new ideas. A recent one is the "can catcher." This is a net on the side of country roads that is specially designed so that walkers, bicyclists, and particularly car drivers can throw their garbage into it. In many countries, drivers often throw garbage into the bushes and grass! Since most people in the Netherlands love to exercise in the country, it is important to keep our countryside clean and tidy.

Traffic congestion

The Netherlands is a densely populated country with a high percentage of car owners. Traffic jams are a major problem, especially in the Randstad, the name given to the region that includes the major cities of Amsterdam, Rotterdam, The Hague, and Utrecht. The government is finding some solutions by creating a very efficient public transportation system of streetcars, trains, and buses. Since vehicles have been banned from the centers of many cities, towns, and villages, people mainly use bicycles to get around. Still, much more can be done to ease traffic congestion.

▲ *Although the roads are busy, the volume of traffic would be greater without the good public transportation system.*

Air pollution

Lead gasoline is no longer sold, and coal is no longer used to heat people's homes. Much of the transportation system is powered by electricity, which is less polluting than diesel or gasoline. However, air pollution remains a problem. The main culprits are the many traffic jams, jet aircraft overhead, gas-burning power stations, factories, and, finally, the pollution that drifts in from neighboring countries.

Water pollution

The Netherlands has severe problems with water pollution. Large contaminated rivers flow into the country, but the Dutch make every effort to clean polluted and waste waters. The excessive use of chemical fertilizers in farming leads to nitrate contamination. Also, the livestock industry produces almost 100 million tons of animal manure a year. Manure puts nitrogen into the soil and the groundwater, which in small quantities is good for the fertility of plants. However,

▲ *Schiphol International Airport is the Netherlands's main international airport, and it is among the busiest in Europe. There are also airports, which cause air pollution, in most towns and cities.*

◄ Many Dutch factories, which use river water for cooling machinery, actually have found that water is cleaner when it leaves the plant than when it arrives. Much of the pollution seen in the Netherlands arrives from elsewhere.

in large doses it becomes toxic, killing plant life and destroying the general environment. Being one of the most densely populated countries in the world does take its toll. The larger the population, the more pollutants and waste water are produced. The smaller the area, the more severe these problems become.

IN THEIR OWN WORDS

My name is Maria Sumaryanto. I am 54 years old and work in Dordrecht. My husband and I don't see any point in getting a car. Here in the Netherlands, the transportation system is very good. I go to work on my bicycle—good for my health and more economical. All around Dordrecht there are rivers and canals, and many people use the fast ferries. My husband works at Schiphol Airport. This is quite far—nearly 100 miles by road there and back. On the train, it takes just over an hour one-way. In nearby Rotterdam, there are the streetcars and the European high-speed train. People are beginning to change. They realize that you do not need a car here.

Conserving the cities

Even though the Dutch love the countryside, their gardens, and their animals, most are city dwellers. Limited space has forced them into building large apartment buildings, but efforts are made to ensure that modern building projects do not spoil the appearance of the many beautiful old towns and cities. Home buyers can choose from the steep-staired traditional Dutch houses, modern detached and semi-detached houses, or houseboats, which line rivers and canals throughout the country.

▲ *Barges used as homes are popular places to live.*

Protecting the countryside

The Dutch have also tried to avoid large-scale building developments in the countryside, where there are quaint old farmhouses, tollhouses, and windmills. Still, conserving natural environments in the Netherlands has not been easy because of the dense population and the pressure on land. Great care has been taken to preserve country areas such as the Drielandenpunt and the Sint Pietersberg hills in Limburg, which have a rural charm of their own. Also conserved are beautiful lakeland areas such as Loosdrechtseplassen and Reeuwijkseplassen, as well as the sand dunes of the North Sea coast, which have been strengthened as natural sea defenses.

▶ *The scenery in the Biesbosch National Park is one of the stunning natural resources of the Netherlands.*

The Hoge Veluwe National Park in the east of the country, with its sand and heathland, is a haven for wildlife. Another national park is the Biesbosch National Park, 17,300 acres (7,000 hectares) of delta near Dordrecht. Finally, there are the mudflats and delta areas of Zeeland, which are important reserves for migrating birds.

▶ *At the Seal Sanctuary on the Wadden island of Texel, North Sea—one of two sanctuaries— seals that are diseased or injured are cared for. Most are eventually returned to the wild.*

IN THEIR OWN WORDS

I'm Elke Koster. I am 30 and work at the Seal Sanctuary at Pieterburen on the Waddenzee coast. Our organization has contacts all along the Dutch coastline and in the Frisian Islands. They locate seals in distress, and they bring them to us at Pieterburen. Seals in the North Sea suffer in many ways. Many are injured by passing ships in one of the busiest, most polluted seaways in the world. Seals also suffer from viruses and disease.

Many tourists come and visit us here to see the seals and our hospital where we treat them. We often have baby seals that have been washed up on the beaches during the winter storms, which in the North Sea can be very severe.

6

The Changing Population

The most noticeable change in the population of the Netherlands over the last few decades is family size; families are getting smaller. There are several reasons for this. Most women now work outside the home and choose to have fewer children so that they can combine family life with a career. Also, since bringing up children can be expensive, people choose to have fewer children so that they can afford to maintain a good standard of living.

The other great change is that people are living to a much older age. A likely reason for this is an excellent health system. The high standard of living is also an important factor: In general, people have good housing, good working conditions, and good diets, all of which help to keep the population healthy into old age.

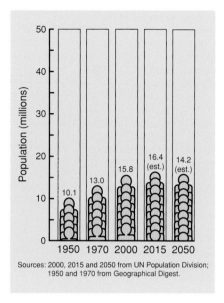

Sources: 2000, 2015 and 2050 from UN Population Division; 1950 and 1970 from Geographical Digest.

▲ *This graph shows that the population of the Netherlands will probably be less in 2050 than it was in 2000.*

◄ *Choosing to have a career before a family is now a common option for women.*

Caring for the aging population

The effect of the fall in family size and increased life expectancy is that there are fewer young people and many more in the elderly age group. This may cause serious problems for the country in the future, since the health care and social benefits provided by the government are paid for by taxes collected from working people. The cost of caring for the aging population is increasing, but the number of young people at work and paying taxes is falling. The government is trying to tackle this problem by reducing the health and social benefits it provides. It is also trying to increase the size of the working population by bringing in workers from overseas.

▶ *There are not enough trained nurses and doctors. Many nurses and doctors now come from African and Asian countries.*

IN THEIR OWN WORDS

I'm Koen van der Bogt. I'm 21 years old and come from Nieuwkoop. I am studying medicine at the University of Leiden. It takes four years to become a doctor before one specializes. To become a surgeon it takes a total of ten years. I haven't decided which branch of medicine I would like to follow—maybe I will go into geriatrics, which is caring for old people. There will be more and more need for specialists in this field as our population gets older and older. Generally there are too few doctors and nurses in the Netherlands, and their pay has not kept up with other professions, so doctors are not happy at the moment.

Immigration

Over 80 percent of the population of the Netherlands is of Dutch origin, but since World War II immigrants have come to the country from many different regions of the world. In the 1940s and 1950s most immigrants came from the former Dutch colonies of Indonesia and Surinam, as well as from the Netherlands Antilles. In the 1950s immigrants started arriving from Italy and Spain, but many of them returned to their homeland, often after retirement. The 1970s saw the arrival of Turkish and Moroccan immigrants, many of whom decided to stay. In the 1980s and 1990s there was an influx of people from Eastern Europe. Recently immigrants have been arriving from countries as diverse as Algeria, Iraq, Pakistan, Rwanda, Ethiopia, and the former Soviet republics. Out of a population of over sixteen million, there are just under three million immigrants.

▼ *There is a large Muslim community, mainly of Turkish and North African origin, living throughout the Netherlands. Here, a large group of Turkish immigrants buy material at a market stall.*

IN THEIR OWN WORDS

My name is Maria Soerjaman. I am 19 and I work in an office at Breda in Brabant. My grandparents are Indonesian. They emigrated to Surinam in South America, then a Dutch colony. I was born in Surinam. Then my family emigrated once again, this time to Holland. Indonesian families have been in the Netherlands such a long time now that we are considered Dutch. I have never had any problems being Indonesian, but maybe that is because I live in a middle-class town. Racism is supposed to be on the increase in cities with a large Muslim population. However, the Netherlands is generally a successfully integrated multiracial society. Many of the famous Dutch soccer players are from the ethnic minorities.

There are now 40,000 legal immigrants who come to the Netherlands annually, but many more arrive illegally. Because of strict controls in the workplace, most of these illegal immigrants are unable to find work and eventually leave for other European Union countries, where it is easier to find asylum and work. Those who stay legally are boosting a declining population, since their families are traditionally larger. Race relations in the Netherlands are better than in most of the neighboring European countries.

▶ *This is Rotterdam's largest mosque, the Mevlana mosque, on the west side of the city. Here Rotterdam's Turkish and North African communities congregate for prayers.*

7

Changes at Home

Changes in family life

As recently as 1970 wives in many Dutch families looked after the home and the family. Now more and more women work outside the home, and the husband and wife share household tasks.

The divorce rate in the Netherlands has shot up in the last twenty years, as it has in much of the developed world, and it is now one of the highest in the world. It is particularly high among people over 50. Economic independence and a desire for a free lifestyle are contributing factors. Possibly because the idea of family is still a very important concept in this country, people often choose to divorce after their children leave home.

There is an increase in single-parent families, but in the Netherlands this is mainly caused by divorces and not by teenage pregnancies, as in many other developed countries. The teenage pregnancy rate is said to be much lower than that of other countries due to the excellent school-based sex education program.

More and more people are deciding simply to live together and not marry at all. Some marry at a much later age, or when they choose to have children.

▲ *There are more single parents in the Netherlands than there used to be.*

◄ *A family on a bicycling trip at Nes on Ameland, one of the Frisian Islands. This is a popular vacation destination with families who have small children, since there are bicycle paths, bicycle traffic lights, and free bike-parking areas.*

High housing prices

The price of houses in the Netherlands has risen so much that young people find it very difficult to afford their first home. Even couples who are both working have difficulty getting a mortgage. As a result, young working adults often live with their parents until they are able to buy their own house or afford a reasonable rent.

There have always been government controls on the rents that landlords can charge, which keeps most rented housing affordable. It is not uncommon for Dutch people to rent for their entire life.

▶ *This is a typical apartment building in Breda, a small town in North Brabant. In recent years house prices have increased dramatically throughout the Netherlands.*

IN THEIR OWN WORDS

My name is Leo Duitsch and I was born in the city of Groningen in the Netherlands. My parents emigrated to Australia when I was 17 years old. My mom and dad then divorced. I decided to go back to the Netherlands for a vacation. I had such a great time that I decided to stay, even though I was far away from my family. I now own my own business, a typical Dutch snack bar. It is only a few streets away from where I was born! My father has also returned to the Netherlands.

Health issues

The Dutch health system is highly regarded. Everyone must have medical insurance, either from the state or private companies. Hospitals are excellent. Generally the Dutch people are fairly fit, as shown by their high life expectancy. People in all age groups use bicycles to get around, which helps to keep them healthy. However, their intake of dairy foods, French fries, and meat means that there is heart disease. Also, the high consumption of tobacco and alcohol causes serious medical problems.

Eating habits

Despite such problems, traditional Dutch family meals are generally varied and healthy. At breakfast the table is set with many kinds of bread, butter, boiled eggs, cold meats, cheeses, chocolate bits (*hagelslag*), preserves, and even chocolate spread. There is always a pot of hot, strong coffee. Traditionally, lunch was the largest meal, but this has changed over the years, since modern people tend to work in office jobs, which do not require heavy meals in preparation for physical work. Now, lunch is similar to breakfast. The early evening meal is the largest meal of the day, often including a large plate of stewed meat with vegetables and applesauce, followed by dessert.

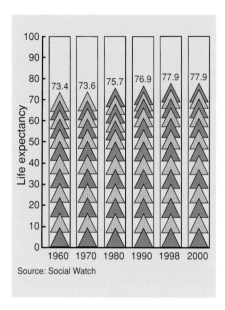

Source: Social Watch

▲ *This graph shows that life expectancy in the Netherlands is high.*

◄ *Street cafés in Amsterdam are very popular. A typical snack would be an* Uitsmijter *(an open sandwich served with a fried egg on top).*

Eating out might involve eating a whole cured raw herring in the marketplace, with possibly some smoked eels or gray shrimp. There are also many kinds of sandwiches, called *broodjes*. Cakes and coffee are always a favorite. Going out to a restaurant often means going for an Italian meal or having a *rijsttafel* (an assortment of specialities from Southeast Asia) in a local Indonesian restaurant. American fast-food restaurants and the snackbar (or *friettent)*, a local shop serving French fries and a range of factory-made snacks, are also popular.

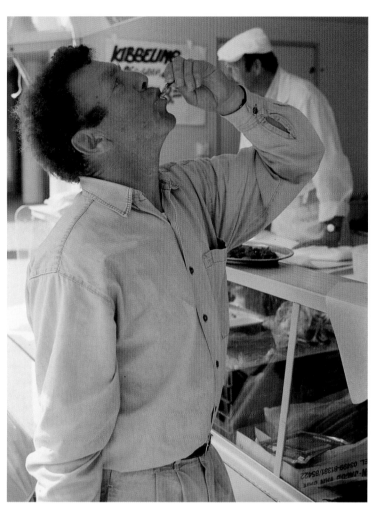

▶ *A favorite Dutch snack is to eat a cured raw herring—swallowed whole. Other seafood favorites are eels, gray shrimp, calamari, mussels, and smoked fish.*

IN THEIR OWN WORDS

I am Surinder Kumar and am 45 years old. I am a Sikh from India. I have been living in the Netherlands for twenty years. For the last nine years I have owned an Indian restaurant in Breda, specializing in Indian and Surinam dishes. We decided to make Surinam dishes, too, because of the large number of Surinam people who live here in Breda. Surinam people are mixed race, black, white, Indian, and Indonesian peoples. They love roti—meat in a huge dough envelope. My restaurant is always busy; we do a lot of take-out business for students and families.

Education

The Netherlands has a system of tracked education, which means that students are put into separate schools depending on their intellectual abilities. This educational system generally achieves high standards. Students from four to twelve years of age attend primary school. After primary school, students are tested, and their results determine what type of secondary school they attend.

Some students enter schools that prepare them for technical schools (to study anything from hairdressing to car maintenance). Apprenticeship remains a crucial part of this vocational education, since students learn how to work in a specific industry while still studying at school. For example, a building student will study for four days and work for two days on a construction site. Other students enter a general school, which gives a good overall education. This is for students who are not aiming at further education or want to enter the workforce as soon as possible without any specialization. Finally, other students attend a school that eventually prepares students for college. Further education is available at 14 regular universities, 50 universities of professional education, and 15 international education institutes, where all courses are conducted in English.

▲ *The number of students attending college, such as this one at Leiden, has risen in recent years.*

◄ *A professor in car mechanics at a technical school in Wyck teaches a student car maintenance.*

English is very important as a second language. Dutch teenagers use many English words in their daily vocabulary. In some European countries, especially France and Germany, there is concern about the increasing use of English, which is seen as a threat to the national culture and language. However, it is not generally regarded as a problem in the Netherlands. Most Dutch people speak English with some fluency, and they often speak several languages. At school everyone studies English and at least one other European language, usually French or German. The Dutch are usually better at German, since Dutch and German are similar in many ways.

▶ *Three friends at Groningen University return from an English Language Club to their apartments in the city.*

IN THEIR OWN WORDS

My name is Stephan van Keulen. I am 19 and I come from Den Helder in North Holland. I want to study computer science at the Delft University, one of the best in the world, and then go on to study advanced computer studies in the United States. I already have my own business. At 14 I worked at a local computer shop, and then two years later I started my own business designing websites. My parents are both computer literate, and they helped me get started. My father is in the Navy and mom runs my office. Computers have changed the way we live in the Netherlands. My business has made quite a lot of money. This will help me during my studies in Delft and the United States.

Religion

Christianity is the main religion, and for centuries the country has been divided into the mainly Catholic south and mostly Protestant north. The number of people belonging to either religion has fallen, however, and many Dutch people are now indifferent to religion of any kind. Some have started following religious sects such as Hare Krishna. Immigrants have brought new religious influences into the country. There are more than 500,000 practicing Muslims, and most large cities have at least one mosque.

Amsterdam once had one of the largest Jewish communities in Europe, but almost the entire Jewish population of the Netherlands (some 140,000 people) was wiped out during the Nazi occupation in World War II. Today, many Jews have returned to areas of Amsterdam. Anne Frank, the teenage Jewish girl who wrote a famous diary while hiding from the Nazis, lived in Amsterdam, and the house where she and her family lived in secret can be visited.

▲ Dutch Hare Krishna followers being married in a Hare Krishna temple in neighboring Belgium.

Festivals, sports, and leisure

There are many festivals in the Netherlands, such as Queen's Day on April 30. In Zeeland and Friesland medieval Ringrijden festivals, in which people ride on horseback along a track and spear a small ring with a lance, are popular. National sports include speed skating and soccer. Dutch speed skaters

◄ This is part of the traditional Ringrijden competitions in Middelburg Zeeland.

arc among the top in the world, and soccer players play in teams all over the world. Ice skating and cycling are also popular sports, as are windsurfing, swimming, and sailing.

The computer has altered Dutch home life. Electronic games are very popular, and people of all ages spend a lot of time on the Internet. Over 90 percent of all homes have a computer.

▲ *The spring Lenten carnival at Maastricht takes place in the southern Netherlands in the predominantly Christian provinces.*

IN THEIR OWN WORDS

My name is Jantiena Dijkstra and I am a psychology student. I come from Oude-Bildtzijl in Friesland. Most of the people in the area speak Frisian, which is considered to be the closest language to English. Since the age of six, I have played an old traditional Frisian ball game called *Kaats*. The game is played on a field by teams of three players, one server, and two field players. The ball is hit with the hand. But we of course wear gloves. Each time the ball is returned to a specific point, *kaatsen* are scored. That is how the game is won or lost. We have matches on the weekends in different villages.

8

Changes at Work

Industrial production

Some of the traditional industries for which the Netherlands is famous, such as diamond cutting in Amsterdam and high-quality porcelain production at Delft, continue to thrive in the modern economy. An important industrial activity is the production of secondary products—in other words, any product made out of an imported primary product. Primary products such as crude oil, iron, and wheat, for example, are turned into secondary products such as gasoline, steel, and bread. Secondary products include computers, jet engines, roasted and packed Columbian coffee beans, and cosmetics made from imported fish oils. Secondary products are now the second biggest income earner after gas and oil. There has been a shift into more automated industries and into a large national and international service sector.

▲ *A porcelain and ceramics stall in the market at Delft. Antique Delft porcelain is highly priced in auctions throughout the world.*

One of the reasons for the Netherlands' economic success is the "poldermodel" of industrial relations. This is a term describing the civilized way in which government, management, and workforce resolve disputes and plan together for the future. Dutch companies such as Philips, Shell, Unilever, ING, ABN-Amro, Fokker, KLM, Elsevier, and C&A are famous worldwide and provide ample proof of the success of Dutch business.

▶ *Unilever's headquarters (the round tower) in Rotterdam. The Netherlands has a strong position in world trade.*

IN THEIR OWN WORDS

My name is Con Bracke, and I am 44 years old. I have worked at one of the Philips plants in Eindhoven for several years. I am a DVD software test engineer for their consumer electronic branch. As an employee of the company I have many benefits. I can use the plant's own sports center and fitness club. We earn generally good salaries and have good job security . . . but for how long? These days Philips is moving a lot of production elsewhere in the world, where labor costs are cheaper. We have a famous local soccer team, PSV Eindhoven, who are sponsored by Philips—their stadium is called the "Philips Stadium."

Europoort

Rotterdam's Europoort has had a very significant effect on the economy of the Netherlands. This port facility of some 8,800 acres (3,560 hectares), which was built between 1958 and 1978, is the largest in the world. There are five oil refineries in the Europoort alone. It is a highly efficient port, turning around the largest tonnage in the shortest time. It has attracted much business and industry to the Netherlands, such as shipping, trucking, and transportation.

◄ *A fuel barge travels through the Calland Channel in the Europoort industrial harbor complex, which is the largest in the world.*

Changes in the country

Farming practices are changing rapidly. Most small, efficient family-owned farms have become highly automated, and wind power is being used widely. One wind turbine can produce a farm's entire energy requirements. Also, computers have become important tools for farmers for managing, planning, and selling their stock and products.

Since the 1990s the Dutch livestock industry has been hit by several outbreaks of animal diseases. There are concerns that intensive farming methods, in which animals are kept close together and raised as quickly as possible, have contributed to this problem. More farmers are trying to farm in ways that cause less damage to the environment and produce healthier livestock, although this tends to be a more expensive way to farm. Giant food businesses continue to pay less for farm produce, causing many to feel that it is impossible to sustain safe farming practices.

▼ *There is an increase in organic farming methods due to the number of animal diseases seen in recent years.*

Tourism

Tourism is important in the Netherlands. Amsterdam, with its tree-lined canals, beautiful old buildings, museums, and exciting nightlife, brings in millions of tourists annually. But there are many other beautiful historic towns such as Leiden, Delft, Utrecht, Enkhuizen, Haarlem, Zierikzee, Urk, Groningen, and Maastricht. Many come to visit the magnificent tulip gardens at the Keukenhof and the flower auctions at Aalsmeer. Some also come to the famous cheese market at Alkmaar.

▼ *Men in colorful costumes carry huge cheeses on wooden sleighs to be weighed and then sold in the Town Square at Edam. The famous cheeses sell throughout the world.*

◀ *A tour boat on the Oude Schans canal in Amsterdam's picturesque "Venice of the North" central area. People from all over the world visit this exciting city.*

Farmers are looking to tourism for new ways to make their businesses profitable. They now organize cycling vacations, with bed-and-breakfasts at old Dutch farmhouses and converted windmills, as well as canal and river trips across rural Holland.

▶ *This graph shows that the number of agricultural workers from 1980 to 2000 halved due to big changes in farming pracices.*

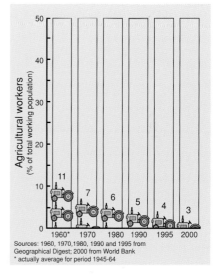

Sources: 1960, 1970,1980, 1990 and 1995 from Geographical Digest; 2000 from World Bank
* actually average for period 1945-64

IN THEIR OWN WORDS

My name is Linda Pluimers and I'm 39. I work at one of the many bike rental shops in Amsterdam. I have worked here for three-and-a-half years now. It's a lot of fun. I think that the center of Amsterdam should be completely free of motor vehicles. Already much of it is. Bicycles are a way of life here—I don't know anyone who doesn't have one. Now all the tourists rent bicycles, because they have realized it is the best way to visit our city. Amsterdam is a great city for having fun. Maybe that is why we get so many tourists from all over the world.

Changes to working life

Great changes are happening in the workplace. Since the 1990s some industrial production has been moved to countries where workers' wages and raw materials are cheaper and taxes are lower. This is a change that has affected industries in many countries. However, the Dutch economy has dealt with this change surprisingly well. The "poldermodel" again succeeded, and the workforce agreed to have their wages frozen. In fact the country has retained one of the lowest unemployment rates in the world. Very recently there has been a dramatic economic downturn, and so time will tell if the "poldermodel" will work this time.

▲ *Clog making is a traditional industry that is still thriving today because of the tourist trade.*

IN THEIR OWN WORDS

I'm Marisca Kensenhuis and I was born in Surinam. This used to be a Dutch colony in South America. I'm 32 years old and live in Amsterdam. I am a part-time flight attendant for KLM, so I visit the entire world. I also work in a café in old Amsterdam, mainly on the weekends. I love it there because of the great atmosphere, especially when the weather is good. On top of all this, I also study communication management full-time. I would like to be a copywriter or journalist or work in Dutch television. That would probably mean moving to Hilversum, the town where all the television studios are located.

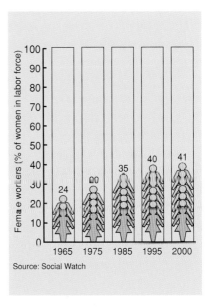

The government has reduced subsidies that previously allowed people to spend long years in higher education, and so many more people are now in the workforce. People used to work in the same job for twenty years or more, but they have now begun to move frequently between companies to get a better salary. Everyone is increasingly mobile, and much work is part time. Many people feel this might undermine the traditional reliability of Dutch business.

Since 1970 more and more women have joined the workforce. However, 80 percent of all key jobs are still held by men, and women's wages are lower on average than their male colleagues. Many women in the Netherlands still opt for staying at home during the first few years of the children's upbringing, which can affect their career opportunities in later life.

Source: Social Watch

▲ *This graph shows that the number of women employed in the Netherlands has risen steadily since 1965.*

▼ *The number of women who work is increasing, despite the fact that many men have higher-paid jobs with more responsibility.*

New businesses

One positive outcome of the instability in the workplace is the opening of many new businesses. People who have worked for the same company for several years are often given large severance payments when they are laid off, and some choose to invest the money in new businesses. Opening a business has never been easy in the Netherlands. To start with, people have to have diplomas in accounting, and then a diploma in the type of business they wish to conduct—for example, in hairdressing, or in food management for a snack bar. These rules ensure that customers receive a high standard of service.

The Netherlands has become a very computer literate, multilingual society. Both multilingualism and, particularly, computer technology have generated vast industries of their own: translation services, language schools, and Internet-based companies.

▲ Skyscrapers are part of the business heart of The Hague. Throughout its history the Netherlands has been an important trading power. It is still a powerful trading nation today.

IN THEIR OWN WORDS

I am Yue Yan Wu and I am a Dutch national. I was born in China. I am a co-owner with my brother of a typical Dutch snackbar, or *frituur*, as it is called down here in Limburg. My parents own a Chinese restaurant in Meersen. We are breaking with family tradition and cook Dutch snacks and, of course, French fries. We first emigrated to Europe when I was twelve. That was to Italy. Then, when I was seventeen, our family moved to the Netherlands. So I speak Italian, Dutch, English, Putonghua Chinese, and our own Wencheng dialect. Since we are near the German border, I am also learning German.

▲ *This Information Officer chooses images for a magazine. They will be scanned digitally. The layout of the magazine is done entirely by computer.*

European markets

The gap between European nations is closing fast, not only in practical terms such as laws and taxes, but also in the way they view each other. Most of the Dutch workforce is very highly skilled, confident in using information technology, and able to speak other European languages. The Dutch are therefore more prepared than most to take advantage of new job opportunities across the expanding European Union. The introduction of the single European currency, the euro, has made it even easier for businesses to operate across Europe. The Dutch are perhaps the most pro-euro of all European nations.

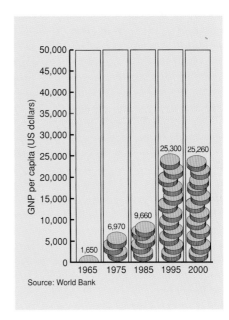

Source: World Bank

▶ *This graph shows that the Dutch national income has risen since 1995. One reason for this is money made from gas and oil supplies.*

9

The Way Ahead

The Netherlands is a country that has fully embraced the European Union and its currency the euro, believing it to be essential for the future of an economically strong Europe. It is also in favor of closer cooperation among the countries of Europe. This closer union could finally bring the countries of Europe together in a new "continent-country." The hope is that this will ensure peace and stability for the future of the continent.

One consequence of the move toward closer European integration might be that the characteristics of individual countries become diluted. It is even possible that languages such as Dutch will be replaced by a common language such as English for business purposes, with Dutch spoken only at home. On the whole, however, European union is seen as offering positive opportunities for Dutch people and the Dutch economy. The Netherlands and its Europoort will profit in terms of trade, since other countries that are planning to become part of the new Europe do not have the facilities

▲ *Young people relax outside the famous Boymans-Van Beuningen Museum in central Rotterdam. Some of the greatest painters in the world have been Dutch, including Vincent van Gogh.*

◀ *The Dutch enjoy different styles of music from all over the world.*

IN THEIR OWN WORDS

I'm Nathaly Archontaki. I'm 14 and I live in Maastricht with my mother. My grandparents live next door. My family is a living example of the European Union. My father is Greek, my grandfather is Spanish, and my grandmother is Dutch. I speak four languages: English, Dutch, French, and Spanish. I also speak the local Maastricht dialect. My hobby is flamenco dancing. I love it. Many Dutch people like it, too. My grandfather emigrated from Andalusia in Spain to work in the coal mines here. Then they all closed, and after some other jobs, he and my grandmother opened a very successful tapas restaurant in the city. I want to become a European television presenter, broadcasting right across Europe, from Dublin to Kiev.

of the Rotterdam port. Already countries such as Poland, the Czech Republic, Slovakia, and the Baltic States are transporting their exports via the Netherlands. The future looks very bright for this country. The Netherlands is at the heart of Europe, with an eye on the wider world. It is a country that has changed in the past, and it is ready to adapt to change in the future.

▼ *This is part of the "Zeeland Delta Project." In times of high tides and storms, the locks close so that the sea is held back.*

Glossary

apprenticeship period of time a person spends learning a skill or trade

automated industries industries in which many or all of the processes are carried out by machines instead of people

colony country that is occupied and politically controlled by another country or countries

estuary mouth of a river where it flows into the ocean or sea

European Economic Community organization set up to promote trade links among some of the countries in Western Europe

European Union group of European countries that work together to achieve economic and social progress and strengthen Europe's role in the world

exports goods that are sold abroad

genetically engineered crops crops that have had their basic genetic makeup changed in some way, for example, to make them more resistant to disease or produce a bigger crop

GNP (gross national product) total value of all the goods and services a country produces in a year, including investments in the country by other nations

horticulture science of growing fruits, vegetables, flowers, and decorative plants

immigrant person who has come to live in a country from another country

imports goods that are bought from other countries

jetty pier that reaches into the sea to protect a harbor or direct the current. It can also be used for docking boats.

life expectancy average length of time that people can expect to live

mortgage money that is borrowed from a bank in order to buy a house

multilingual using or being able to use several different languages

NATO (North Atlantic Treaty Organization) organization set up by the United States and Western European countries after World War II to defend the West against the military threat that existed at that time from the Soviet Union

organic food produced without the use of chemicals

polder land that was once under the sea but that has been drained so that it can be farmed or built upon

poldermodel Dutch way of doing business that emphasizes respect for other people

porcelain type of fine china

service sector businesses such as restaurants, banks, and stores that provide services to customers

subsidies money that is paid by the government to reduce the cost of something, for example, producing goods

trawler person who catches fish using a trawl, a cone-shaped net that is dragged along the bottom of the water

Further Information

Books

Bolt, Rodney. *Take the Kids to Amsterdam, with Trips Around Holland.* London: Cadogan Guides, 2000.

Greenberg, Jan. *Vincent van Gogh: Portrait of an Artist.* Toronto: Dell, 2003.

Rubin, Susan Goldman. *Searching for Anne Frank: Letters from Amsterdam to Iowa.* New York: Harry N. Abrams, 2003.

Useful Addresses

The Netherlands Embassy, Washington, D.C.
4200 Linnean Avenue NW
Washington, DC, 20008
202-244-5300
www.netherlands-embassy.org

Embassy of the United States
The Hague, the Netherlands
thehague.usembassy.gov

Index

Page numbers in **bold** refer to pages with photographs, maps, or statistics panels.